Learning
From Home
for Primary

Ages 3+

Practice for children with Pen Control, Line Tracing, Letters and More!

K.K. & T Creations

FAMILY LEARNING PUBLISHING

AF448016

A a

B b

B
B

b
b

C c

C
c

Dd

D

D D D D D D D

D D D D D D D

d

d d d d d d d

d d d d d d d

E e

e

Ff

F

f

Gg

Name:_______________________

Hh

H

h

Name:
Ii

Jj

Name:_______________________

Kk

K

k

L l

Mm

Name:________________________________

Nn

Name:

Pp

Name:_______________________________

R r

Ss

T t

Name:

Name:

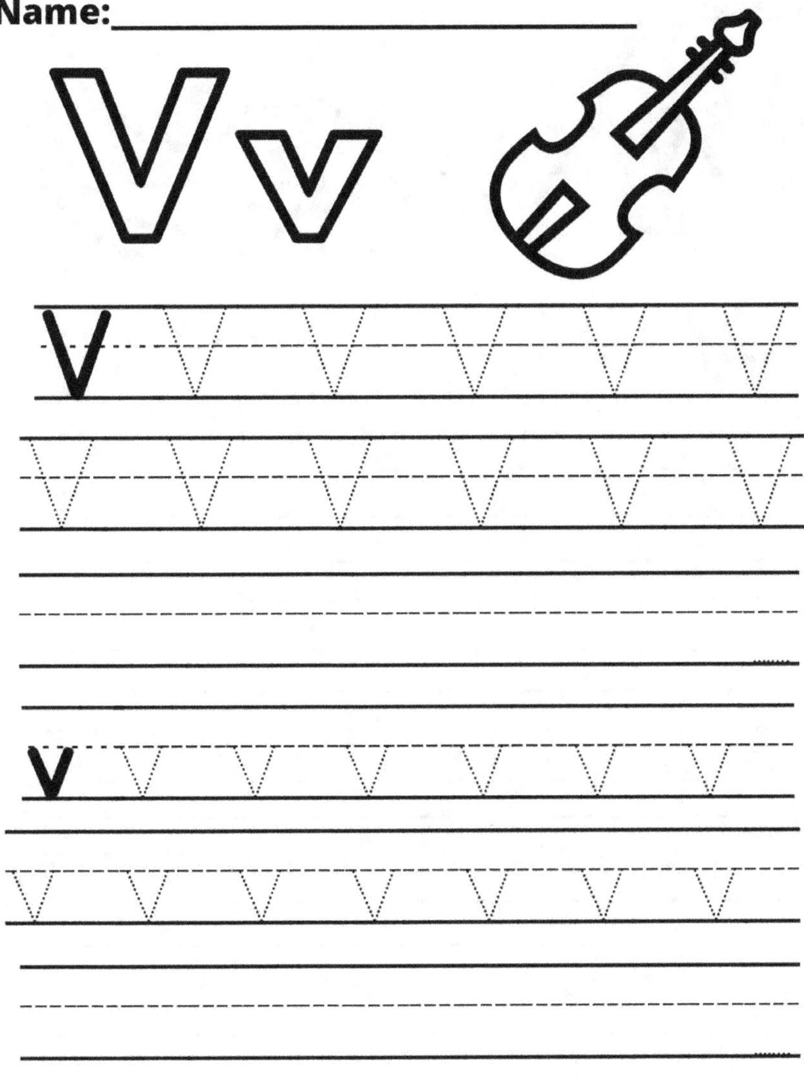

Name:

W w

W

w

Xx

Name:___________________________

Y y

Zz